contents

British & North American Readers:
Please note that Australian cup and
spoon measurements are metric. A quick
conversion guide appears on page 63.
A glossary explaining unfamiliar terms
and ingredients begins on page 60.

2   all about chicken

Chicken is a universal favourite: its very mildness of flavour makes it a crowd-pleaser. It can stand on its own as a simple roast or it can be used as the perfect foil for spicy and pungent flavours. And it's easy to prepare too – follow these simple instructions and you can't go wrong.

Preparing chicken

First check that there's not a plastic bag inside the chicken containing the giblets. If there is, remove it (give the giblets to the cat or use them to make a gravy). Remove the neck and any pieces of fat. Rinse the chicken inside and out under cold water and pat dry with absorbent paper. Now it's ready for cooking, unless you want to truss it (trussing a chicken, ie, tying its legs together and tucking its wings under, helps it keep its shape – important if carving at the table). When using chicken breast fillets, remove the silvery tendon that runs down the middle and cut off any fat.

Frozen chicken

When you buy a frozen chicken, get it home quickly (or take an insulated container with you to the supermarket). If it starts to thaw out, don't re-freeze it. Rather, unwrap it, put it on a plate, cover it loosely with plastic or foil and thaw it in the refrigerator – it will take about 24 hours. Don't ever re-freeze thawed chicken — or any other frozen food for that matter.

What's in a name?

In most English-speaking countries, a spatchcock means a chicken (or game bird) that's been split down the back, flattened out and grilled. It can refer to any size chicken. In Australia, it has come to mean a small chicken, usually weighing between 300–600g, which may or may not be split and flattened. Elsewhere this small bird is called a poussin, baby chicken or squab chicken.

Safe chicken

Chicken has unfairly gained a reputation for being a "dangerous" food in terms of causing food poisoning. But chicken is no more unsafe than any other food if you follow these rules of hygiene:

• Wash your hands before preparing food.

• Keep raw and cooked foods separate when storing in the refrigerator. Put everything on plates and cover loosely with foil or plastic, so juices can't drip onto food on a lower shelf.

• Prepare raw and cooked food separately. Once you've finished with one, wash knife, chopping board and hands before you start on the other. Organisms can be transferred easily to a cooked chicken if it is cut on a board that has just held the same cut before it was cooked.

• Cook chicken thoroughly. A whole chicken must be cooked until its internal temperature reaches 75°C or higher. Be very careful to cook chicken mince thoroughly too.

• Once the chicken is cooked, it should be eaten as soon as possible. Or if eating cold, it should be chilled.

• Fresh chicken should be kept in the refrigerator for no more than 3 days before cooking.

• Frozen chicken can be kept in the freezer for 2 months.

Chicken sizes

The size numbers on chickens indicate their weight. Thus a number 10 chicken weighs 1kg; a number 16 chicken weighs l.6kg and so on.

Tips

• Don't baste a roasting chicken too often – it will keep the skin moist and prevent it from crisping. And every time you open the oven door the oven temperature drops.

• Cover the chicken with foil if it's browning too fast.

• When you microwave a chicken the legs and wings will cook faster than the rest of the bird. Cover these extremities tightly with foil and remove halfway through cooking time.

Chicken's favourite herbs

Sage is the classic herb for chicken stuffing, but it can be overpowering so don't use too much. Tarragon is much more subtle, perfect with the mild flavour of chicken. Lemon thyme, more delicate than garden thyme, imparts a mild lemon flavour to chicken dishes. Bay leaves add flavour to chicken casseroles and chervil is a lovely herb to sprinkle over a chicken salad.

4 chicken and wild rice
paella

300g uncooked medium prawns

8 small (120g) mussels

1/3 cup (60g) wild rice

5 (550g) chicken thigh fillets

1 small (200g) leek, chopped

2 cloves garlic, crushed

1 medium (200g) yellow capsicum, ohoppod

1 medium (200g) red capsicum, chopped

1 teaspoon sambal oelek

2 tablespoons chopped fresh thyme

1 cup (200g) basmati rice

1/4 cup (60ml) dry white wine

1/2 teaspoon saffron threads

2 cups (500ml) chicken stock

2 tablespoons drained capers

2 medium (240g) yellow zucchini, chopped

1 tablespoon chopped fresh parsley

Shell and devein prawns, leaving heads and tails intact. Scrub mussels, remove beards. Cook wild rice in small pan of boiling water, uncovered, about 20 minutes or until tender; drain. Rinse wild rice under cold water; drain well.

Cook chicken in heated large non-stick pan until browned both sides and almost cooked through; remove from pan. Drain chicken on absorbent paper; slice chicken.

Add leek, garlic, capsicums, sambal oelek and thyme to same pan, cook, stirring, 5 minutes. Add basmati rice, wine, saffron, stock and chicken; cook, covered, about 12 minutes or until rice is just tender. Add seafood, capers, zucchini and wild rice; cook, covered, further 5 minutes or until seafood is tender. Serve sprinkled with parsley.

Per serve fat 8g; fibre 5g; kj 2134

chicken with
red beans

2 tablespoons water

1 medium (150g) onion, chopped

2 medium (400g) red capsicums, chopped

1 tablespoon sliced canned drained jalapeno peppers

2 cloves garlic, crushed

1/2 teaspoon chilli powder

1 teaspoon sweet paprika

1 teaspoon ground coriander

1 teaspoon ground cumin

750g lean minced chicken

2 x 310g cans red kidney beans, rinsed, drained

425g can tomatoes

2 tablespoons tomato paste

1 tablespoon chopped fresh parsley

Freeze Suitable
Per serve fat 9g; fibre 10g; kj 1546

Combine water, onion, capsicums, peppers and garlic in heated large non-stick pan; cook, stirring, until onion is soft. Stir in chilli powder, paprika, coriander and cumin; cook, stirring, until fragrant. Add chicken; cook, stirring, until browned. Add beans, undrained crushed tomatoes, paste and parsley; simmer, covered, about 15 minutes or until thickened slightly.

mustard and rosemary chicken
with artichokes

3 (500g) chicken
breast fillets, sliced

cooking-oil spray

2 small (200g) red
onions, chopped
roughly

1 clove garlic, crushed

1/2 teaspoon cracked
black pepper

2 teaspoons cornflour

1/2 teaspoon chicken
stock powder

1/2 cup (125ml) water

1/4 cup (60ml) dry
white wine

2 teaspoons seeded
mustard

1 teaspoon
Worcestershire sauce

400g can artichoke
hearts in brine,
drained, quartered

2 teaspoons chopped
fresh rosemary

Per serve fat 4g; fibre 3g;
kj 794

Cook chicken, in batches, in heated oiled large
pan, stirring, until browned both sides and
almost cooked through. Add onions, garlic and
pepper; cook, stirring, until onions are soft.
Return chicken to same pan with blended
cornflour, stock powder and water, wine,
mustard and sauce; stir over heat until mixture
boils and thickens slightly. Add artichokes and
rosemary, stir until hot.

8

chicken and chestnuts in
lettuce cups

5 Chinese dried mushrooms

500g lean minced chicken

cooking-oil spray

1/4 teaspoon sesame oil

1 small (150g) red capsicum, chopped finely

2 cloves garlic, crushed

1 tablespoon grated fresh ginger

230g can bamboo shoots, rinsed, drained, chopped finely

230g can water chestnuts, drained, rinsed, chopped finely

4 green onions, sliced

1 tablespoon soy sauce

1 tablespoon oyster sauce

1 tablespoon dry sherry

1/3 cup (80ml) water

1/2 teaspoon sambal oelek

1 iceberg lettuce

1 tablespoon chopped fresh coriander leaves

Place mushrooms in heatproof bowl, cover with boiling water, stand 20 minutes; drain. Discard stems; finely slice caps.

Cook chicken, in batches, in heated oiled large pan, stirring, until browned and cooked through.

Add sesame oil, capsicum, garlic and ginger to same pan; cook, stirring, until capsicum is soft.

Return chicken to pan with mushrooms, bamboo shoots, chestnuts, onions, sauces, sherry, water and sambal oelek; cook, stirring, until hot. Serve chicken mixture in lettuce cups, sprinkled with chopped coriander.

Per serve fat 7g; fibre 5g; kj 899

dry chicken

curry

2 medium (300g) onions, chopped

cooking-oil spray

6 curry leaves, torn

1 teaspoon cumin seeds

1 teaspoon black mustard seeds

2 cloves garlic, crushed

2 teaspoons grated fresh ginger

1 teaspoon garam masala

1 teaspoon ground turmeric

1/2 teaspoon chilli powder

1 teaspoon salt

750g chicken thigh fillets, halved

1/2 cup (125ml) water

1 tablespoon chopped fresh coriander leaves

Cook onions on heated oiled non-stick pan, stirring, until browned lightly.
Add leaves, seeds, garlic, ginger, ground spices and salt; cook, stirring,
until fragrant. Add chicken, stir well to coat in spice mixture. Add water;
simmer, covered, about 30 minutes or until chicken is tender. Boil,
uncovered, about 15 minutes or until most liquid has evaporated. Just
before serving, stir in coriander.

Freeze Suitable
Per serve fat 9g; fibre 2g; kj 1079

10 chicken COUSCOUS
with spicy tomato sauce

1/4 cup (60ml) water

1 small chicken stock cube, crumbled

1/4 cup (50g) couscous

15g butter

1/2 small (45g) zucchini, grated

1/2 small (35g) carrot, grated

1 tablespoon chopped fresh coriander leaves

4 (680g) chicken breast fillets

1 medium (150g) onion, chopped

425g can tomato puree

1/2 teaspoon ground cumin

1/2 teaspoon ground coriander

1/4 teaspoon chilli powder

1/2 cup (125ml) dry white wine

1/2 cup (125ml) water, extra

2 tablespoons chopped fresh coriander leaves, extra

Bring water and stock cube to boil in small pan, stir in couscous, stand 5 minutes or until water is absorbed. Stir in butter, zucchini, carrot and fresh coriander.

Cut a pocket in thickest side of each fillet. Spoon couscous mixture into each pocket, secure with toothpicks. Cook chicken in heated non-stick pan until browned both sides; remove from pan. Add onion to pan; cook, stirring, until soft. Stir in puree, cumin, coriander, chilli powder, wine and extra water; simmer, uncovered, 5 minutes. Return chicken to pan, simmer, uncovered, further 10 minutes. Stir in extra fresh coriander. Remove toothpicks, serve chicken sliced with sauce.

Per serve fat 8g; fibre 4g; kj 1398

warm chicken, ham
and mushroom salad

Boil, steam or microwave beans until just tender, rinse under cold water; drain. Cut ham into thin strips.

Cook garlic and chicken in heated oiled large pan until chicken is browned both sides and cooked through. Remove chicken from pan; slice thinly.

Cook onions, mushrooms and mustard in heated oiled small pan, stirring, until onions are soft. Add ham; stir until heated through.

Toss beans, lettuce and endive with dressing, top with chicken and hot ham and mustard mixture.

Microwave Beans suitable

Per serve fat 6g; fibre 4g; kj 1117

100g green beans, sliced

100g sliced smoked ham

2 cloves garlic, crushed

4 (680g) chicken breast fillets

cooking-oil spray

4 green onions, chopped

125g button mushrooms, chopped finely

2 tablespoons seeded mustard

1 medium coral lettuce

300g curly endive

1/4 cup (60ml) bottled fat-free French dressing

12 chicken skewers with
tomato rice

You will need to cook about 1/2 cup (100g) rice for this recipe. Soak bamboo skewers in water for 1 hour to prevent burning.

4 (680g) chicken breast fillets

1/4 cup (60ml) low-fat yogurt

1 teaspoon ground coriander

1 teaspoon ground cumin

2 cloves garlic, crushed

1 tablespoon water

1 medium (150g) onion, chopped

2 medium (380g) tomatoes, seeded, chopped

1 1/2 cups cooked white long-grain rice

1/4 cup (40g) chopped dates

2 tablespoons slivered almonds, toasted

1 tablespoon chopped fresh coriander leaves

200g sugar snap peas

Cut chicken into 2cm cubes. Combine chicken with yogurt, coriander, cumin and half the garlic in large bowl; mix well. Thread chicken onto 8 skewers. Grill skewers until chicken is tender. Meanwhile, combine water, onion and remaining garlic in heated large non-stick pan; cook, stirring, until onion is softened. **Add** tomatoes, rice, dates, almonds and coriander; cook, stirring, until heated through.

Boil, steam or microwave peas until just tender; drain. Serve chicken skewers with rice mixture and peas.

Microwave Peas and rice mixture suitable

Per serve fat 7g; fibre 5g; kj 1584

spicy chicken
tacos

2 (340g) chicken
breast fillets

2 tablespoons water

2 medium (300g)
onions, chopped finely

2 cloves garlic,
crushed

2 x 425g cans
tomatoes

1 bottled green
jalapeno pepper,
chopped finely

310g can red kidney
beans, rinsed, drained

8 taco shells

2 cups shredded
iceberg lettuce

1/2 cup (60g) coarsely
grated low-fat cheddar
cheese

Grill or steam chicken until cooked through; cool. Chop chicken finely.
Combine water, onions and garlic in large pan; stir over heat until onions
are soft. Add undrained crushed tomatoes and pepper; simmer,
uncovered, stirring occasionally, until almost all liquid has evaporated.
Stir in chicken and half the beans; mash remaining beans with fork, add
to pan, stir over heat until heated through. Follow packet directions for
heating taco shells. Fill taco shells with lettuce and chicken mixture;
sprinkle with cheese.

Per serve fat 10g; fibre 10g; kj 1374

honey sage chicken 15
with **fruity** seasoning

1.6kg chicken

1 tablespoon soy sauce

1 tablespoon honey

fruity seasoning

1/2 cup (100g) brown rice

1/4 cup (45g) wild rice

1/4 cup (40g) sultanas

1/4 cup (35g) chopped dried apricots

1/4 cup chopped fresh chives

1 tablespoon chopped fresh sage leaves

1 clove garlic, crushed

1 egg white, beaten lightly

sage sauce

1 teaspoon cornflour

1/4 cup (60ml) dry white wine

3/4 cup (180ml) chicken stock

2 teaspoons chopped fresh sage leaves

2 teaspoons Worcestershire sauce

Remove skin and fat from chicken. Fill chicken with Fruity Seasoning, secure opening with skewers. Tie legs together, tuck wings under, place chicken on wire rack in baking dish; brush evenly with some of the combined sauce and honey. Bake, uncovered, in moderate oven about 1 1/2 hours or until chicken is tender, brushing during first half of cooking with honey mixture. Cover legs and wings with foil during cooking if chicken is browning too quickly. Serve chicken with Sage Sauce.

Fruity Seasoning Add brown rice to large pan of boiling water, stir to separate grains, boil, uncovered, 5 minutes. Add wild rice to same pan, stir to separate grains, boil, uncovered, about 20 minutes or until just tender; drain. Combine rices with remaining ingredients; mix well.

Sage Sauce Combine blended cornflour and wine with remaining ingredients in pan; stir over heat until sauce boils and thickens.

Microwave Sage Sauce suitable
Per serve fat 8g; fibre 3g; kj 1753

16 chicken and bean
potatoes

4 large (1.2kg) potatoes

cooking-oil spray

1/4 cup (20g) finely grated parmesan cheese

chicken and bean filling

310g can tomato supreme

310g can red kidney beans, rinsed, drained

2 small (180g) zucchini, sliced

1/2 teaspoon dried mixed herbs

1/4 cup (60ml) water

1 1/2 cups (255g) cooked chopped chicken

Per serve fat 9g; fibre 9g; kj 1658

Prick unpeeled potatoes all over with skewer. Bake in moderately hot oven about 1 hour or until tender. Cut potatoes in half, scoop out flesh, leaving a 1cm thick shell; reserve flesh. Coat potatoes, inside and out with cooking-oil spray. Place onto oven tray, cut-side up; bake in hot oven 10 minutes. Fill potatoes with Chicken and Bean Filling, serve topped with parmesan.

Chicken and Bean Filling Combine tomato supreme, beans, zucchini, herbs and water in medium pan; simmer, covered, about 5 minutes or until zucchini is tender. Chop reserved potato flesh, add to pan with cooked chicken, stir over heat until mixture is heated through.

chicken and artichoke
pies

2 tablespoons dry
white wine

1 cup (250ml) water

2 sticks celery,
chopped

1 tablespoon chopped
fresh oregano

2 medium (300g)
onions, chopped

1 small chicken stock
cube, crumbled

2 tablespoons plain
flour

1 cup (250ml) skim
milk

4 (680g) chicken
breast fillets, chopped

2 x 400g cans
artichoke hearts in
brine, drained, rinsed
chopped

4 sheets fillo pastry

Combine wine, water,
celery, oregano,
onions and stock cube
in pan; simmer,
uncovered, until
onions are soft. Stir in
blended flour and
milk, stir over heat
until mixture boils and
thickens. Stir in
chicken and
artichokes; simmer,
uncovered, about 5
minutes or until
chicken is tender.
Spoon mixture into
four 1½-cup (375ml)
heatproof dishes.
Cut 2 pastry sheets
lengthways into
quarters, cut
remaining sheets
crossways into 8. Roll
strips of pastry,
gathering on one
edge, to form roses,
trim, arrange roses on
top of each pie. Place
pies on oven tray;
bake in moderately hot
oven about 15 minutes
or until pastry is
browned lightly.

Per serve fat 5g; fibre 6g;
kj 1420

18 chive and mustard
chicken

4 (680g) chicken breast fillets

2 teaspoons French mustard

1/2 cup (125ml) water

1 small chicken stock cube, crumbled

2 teaspoons cornflour

2 tablespoons water, extra

1/3 cup (80ml) evaporated skim milk

2 tablespoons chopped fresh chives

Spread chicken with mustard. Cook chicken in large non-stick pan until browned both sides. Add water and stock cube, simmer, uncovered, about 10 minutes or until chicken is tender. Stir in blended cornflour and extra water; stir until sauce boils and thickens. Add milk and chives and stir over heat until hot.

Microwave Suitable
Per serve fat 4g; fibre 0g; kj 901

chicken and

vegetable curry

750g chicken thigh fillets, chopped

cooking-oil spray

1 medium (150g) onion, chopped

4 cloves garlic, crushed

1 large (300g) potato, chopped

2 tablespoons tikka paste

1 tablespoon sambal oelek

1/2 teaspoon cayenne pepper

4 small fresh red chillies, sliced

2 fresh kaffir lime leaves

1 litre (4 cups) chicken stock

2 tablespoons white vinegar

1 tablespoon cornflour

1 tablespoon water

1 medium (200g) red capsicum, chopped

250g broccoli, chopped

1/4 cup firmly packed fresh coriander leaves

Cook chicken in heated oiled large non-stick pan, in batches, until browned all over. Add onion and garlic to pan; cook, stirring, until onion is soft. Return chicken to pan with potato, paste, sambal oelek, cayenne pepper, chillies, leaves, stock and vinegar; simmer, uncovered, about 30 minutes or until potatoes are tender. **Stir** in blended cornflour and water; stir over heat until mixture boils and thickens slightly. Stir in capsicum and broccoli; stir over heat until vegetables are tender. Serve sprinkled with coriander.

Per serve fat 10g; fibre 5g; kj 1451

20 chicken and noodle soup

3 (500g) chicken breast fillets

2 cloves garlic, crushed

3 teaspoons ground cumin

$1/2$ teaspoon ground turmeric

1.5 litres (6 cups) water

2 teaspoons chicken stock powder

1 tablespoon sugar

$1/2$ teaspoon shrimp paste

3 teaspoons sambal oelek

$1/2$ teaspoon grated fresh ginger

50g rice vermicelli noodles

1 cup (80g) bean sprouts

3 lettuce leaves, shredded

2 tablespoons chopped fresh coriander leaves

Cut chicken into 2cm slices. Combine garlic, cumin and turmeric in large pan; stir over heat about 1 minute or until fragrant. Add chicken, water, stock powder, sugar, paste, sambal oelek and ginger; simmer, uncovered, 10 minutes. Add noodles; simmer, uncovered, further 10 minutes. Just before serving, stir in bean sprouts, lettuce and coriander.

Microwave Suitable
Per serve fat 4g; fibre 2g; kj 864

22 chicken with
apricot sauce

4 (680g) chicken
breast fillets

apricot sauce

3cm piece fresh
ginger, peeled

1 cup (250ml) apricot
nectar

3 teaspoons soy
sauce

2 teaspoons cornflour

1 tablespoon water

1 green onion, sliced

Cook chicken in heated large non-stick pan
until browned both sides and cooked through.
Serve chicken with Apricot Sauce.
Apricot Sauce Cut ginger into very thin strips;
combine in pan with nectar, sauce and blended
cornflour and water. Stir over heat, until sauce
boils and thickens. Stir in onion.

Freeze Suitable
Microwave Suitable
Per serve fat 4; fibre 0; kj 971

ginger chilli chicken

with fresh rice noodles

23

Place noodles in bowl, cover with warm water, stand 5 minutes; drain. Heat oil in wok or large pan; stir-fry chicken, in batches until browned and cooked through. Cover to keep warm.

Add eggs to wok, swirl wok so eggs form a thin omelette over base, cook until set. Transfer omelette to board and cut into thin strips.

Add celery to wok; stir-fry until just tender. Add sprouts, onions, garlic, ginger, sauces and stock; stir-fry 2 minutes. Add noodles to wok with chicken and omelette strips; stir-fry until heated and sauce has thickened slightly.

Per serve fat 10g; fibre 3g; kj 1372

500g thick fresh rice noodles

1 tablespoon sesame oil

2 (340g) chicken breast fillets, sliced finely

2 eggs, lightly beaten

2 sticks celery, sliced

1 1/4 cups (100g) bean sprouts

4 green onions, chopped

2 cloves garlic, crushed

2 teaspoons grated fresh ginger

1 tablespoon black bean sauce

2 tablespoons salt-reduced soy sauce

1 tablespoon hot chilli sauce

1 teaspoon fish sauce

1/4 cup (60ml) chicken stock

marinade

4 (680g) chicken breast fillets

2 tablespoons chopped fresh coriander leaves

1 lime

lime chilli marinade

1/3 cup (80ml) lime juice

1 clove garlic, crushed

2 teaspoons grated fresh ginger

1 tablespoon soy sauce

1 small fresh red chilli, chopped finely

2 (50g) spring onions, chopped

Using a meat mallet, flatten chicken breasts to an even thickness. Combine chicken and marinade in large bowl. Cover; refrigerate 3 hours or overnight. Drain chicken; discard marinade.

Cook chicken on heated oiled griddle (or barbecue or grill) until browned both sides and cooked through. Sprinkle with coriander; serve with lime wedges.

Lime Chilli Marinade Combine all ingredients in small bowl; mix well.

Freeze Suitable

Per serve fat 5g; fibre 1g; kj 874

chicken with tomato 25

herb sauce

1/2 cup (125ml) dry white wine or apple juice

1/2 cup (125ml) water

4 (680g) chicken breast fillets

tomato herb sauce

2 large (500g) tomatoes, chopped

1 medium (150g) onion, sliced

2 small chicken stock cubes, crumbled

1 tablespoon chopped fresh basil leaves

1 tablespoon chopped fresh mint leaves

2 tablespoons chopped fresh parsley

1/2 cup (125ml) water

Combine wine and water in large pan; simmer, uncovered, 15 minutes. Add chicken to pan; simmer, uncovered, about 5 minutes or until chicken is cooked through. Drain chicken. Serve chicken with Tomato Herb Sauce.
Tomato Herb Sauce Combine all ingredients in pan; bring to boil, boil, uncovered, 5 minutes.

Microwave Suitable
Per serve fat 4g; fibre 2g; kj 1015

26 minted chicken with sweet
orange sauce

4 (680g) chicken breast fillets

3/4 cup chopped fresh mint

sweet orange sauce

1/2 cup (125ml) white vinegar

1 tablespoon caster sugar

1 cup (250ml) strained orange juice

1 teaspoon cornflour

1 teaspoon water

1 teaspoon butter

Using a meat mallet, flatten chicken breasts to an even thickness. Spread mint over 1 side of chicken breasts, roll up tightly; secure with toothpicks.
Place chicken in heatproof dish, in single layer. Bake, covered, in moderate oven about 25 minutes or until chicken is tender. Remove toothpicks, slice chicken, serve with Sweet Orange Sauce.
Sweet Orange Sauce Combine vinegar and sugar in small pan, stir constantly over heat, without boiling, until sugar is dissolved. Boil, uncovered, without stirring, until mixture turns golden brown. Add juice, simmer, uncovered, until reduced by half. Add blended cornflour and water, stir over heat until sauce boils and thickens. Whisk in butter just before serving.

Per serve fat 5g; fibre 0g; kj 1036

chilli chicken
stir-fry

Combine sauces, honey, vinegar, garlic, ginger and chillies in large bowl, add chicken, mix well. Cover; refrigerate 3 hours or overnight.

Halve onions, cut into wedges. Cut asparagus into 4cm pieces; boil, steam or microwave until just tender; rinse under cold water, drain. Drain chicken from marinade; reserve marinade.

Stir-fry onions in heated oiled large pan until soft. Remove from pan. Add chicken to pan; stir-fry until browned all over. Add marinade; simmer, covered, about 10 minutes or until chicken is cooked through, stirring occasionally. Add onions, bok choy and asparagus; cook, stirring, until bok choy is just wilted.

1 tablespoon mild sweet chilli sauce

2 tablespoons hoisin sauce

2 tablespoons salt-reduced soy sauce

2 tablespoons honey

2 tablespoons rice vinegar

3 cloves garlic, crushed

1 teaspoon grated fresh ginger

3 small fresh red chillies, sliced

800g chicken thigh fillets, quartered

2 large (400g) onions

500g asparagus

cooking-oil spray

500g baby bok choy, shredded

Microwave Asparagus suitable
Per serve fat 10g; fibre 6g; kj 1613

4 (680g) chicken breast fillets

2 cloves garlic, crushed

1 tablespoon lime juice

2 tablespoons chopped fresh coriander leaves

¹/₄ cup chopped fresh mint leaves

2 tablespoons soy sauce

¹/₂ teaspoon sugar

1 medium (200g) red capsicum

1 medium (200g) yellow capsicum

cooking-oil spray

1 baby (60g) eggplant, sliced

2 medium (150g) egg tomatoes, sliced

4 wholegrain bread rolls

dressing

¹/₄ cup (60ml) light sour cream

¹/₄ cup (60ml) low-fat yogurt

2 teaspoons chopped fresh coriander leaves

2 teaspoons chopped fresh mint leaves

1 teaspoon mild sweet chilli sauce

Combine chicken, garlic, juice, herbs, sauce and sugar in large bowl; mix well. Cover; refrigerate 3 hours or overnight.

Quarter capsicums, remove seeds and membranes. Roast under grill or in very hot oven, skin-side up, until skin blisters and blackens. Cover capsicum pieces in plastic or paper for 5 minutes; peel away skin.

Cook chicken on heated oiled griddle (or grill or barbecue) until browned both sides and cooked through. Remove from pan; keep warm. Cook capsicums, eggplant and tomatoes on griddle, turning once, until browned.

Split rolls; toast lightly. Spread rolls with a little Dressing; fill with sliced chicken and vegetables. Serve with remaining Dressing.

Dressing Combine all ingredients in small bowl; mix well.

Per serve fat 10g; fibre 7g; kj 1951

vegetable salad

600g chicken breast fillets

8 cherry tomatoes

5 baby (300g) eggplants

4 small (360g) zucchini

cooking-oil spray

1 tablespoon balsamic vinegar

2 teaspoons fresh thyme leaves

marinade

1/2 cup (125ml) lemon juice

2 cloves garlic, crushed

2 teaspoons olive oil

1 tablespoon chopped fresh thyme

1 tablespoon chopped fresh mint leaves

2 teaspoons caster sugar

Cut chicken into 2cm wide strips. Combine chicken and half the Marinade in large bowl. Cover; refrigerate 3 hours or overnight.
Cut tomatoes into halves. Cut eggplants and zucchini into halves lengthways. Brush vegetables with some of the remaining Marinade, cook in a large oiled non-stick pan until tender. Remove; keep warm.
Drain chicken; discarding its Marinade. Cook in same pan, stirring, until browned and tender. Return vegetables to pan with strained remaining Marinade, vinegar and thyme; stir until heated through.
Marinade Combine all ingredients in bowl.

Per serve fat 7g; 4g; kj 1018

chicken
tikka

6 (1kg) chicken breast
fillets

1 tablespoon grated
fresh ginger

3 cloves garlic,
crushed

2 tablespoons lemon
juice

2 teaspoons ground
coriander

2 teaspoons ground
cumin

1/2 teaspoon garam
masala

1/2 teaspoon chilli
powder

1/3 cup (80ml) low-fat
yogurt

2 tablespoons tomato
paste

pinch tandoori
powdered colour,
optional

Cut chicken fillets in half; make 3 shallow cuts across each piece.
Combine remaining ingredients in large bowl, add chicken; mix well.
Cover; refrigerate overnight. Cook chicken on heated oiled griddle
(or grill or barbecue) until browned both sides and cooked through.

Per serve fat 6g; fibre 2g; kj 1301

32 tomato chicken
risotto

1 medium (200g) red capsicum, quartered

1/2 cup (30g) dry-packed sun-dried tomatoes

1.5 litres (6 cups) chicken stock

2 cups (500ml) tomato juice

1 cup (250ml) dry white wine

5 (550g) chicken thigh fillets, chopped finely

2 cloves garlic, crushed

200g Swiss brown mushrooms, sliced

100g pancetta, chopped

2 cups (400g) arborio rice

1 tablespoon chopped fresh sage

2 teaspoons chopped fresh thyme

Remove seeds and membrane from capsicum. Roast in very hot oven, skin-side up, until skin blackens. Cover in plastic for 5 minutes, peel away skin, finely chop capsicum.

Pour boiling water over tomatoes in bowl, stand 5 minutes; drain. Slice tomatoes thinly.

Combine stock, juice and wine in medium pan, bring to boil; cover, keep hot.

Cook chicken in heated non-stick pan, stirring, until browned; drain. Add garlic, mushrooms and pancetta to pan; cook, stirring, until pancetta is browned. Stir in rice. Add 1 cup (250ml) boiling stock mixture; cook, stirring, until liquid is absorbed. Add chicken, continue adding stock gradually, stirring until absorbed between each addition. Total cooking time should be about 35 minutes. Stir in herbs, capsicum and tomatoes.

Per serve fat 9g; fibre 5g; kj 280

spicy thai-style
chicken

500g lean minced chicken

3 cloves garlic, crushed

6 green onions, chopped

1/3 cup (80ml) mild sweet chilli sauce

500g baby bok choy, chopped

1 tablespoon fish sauce

2 tablespoons salt-reduced soy sauce

2 tablespoons shredded fresh basil leaves

Cook chicken in heated large non-stick pan, stirring, until cooked through. Add garlic, onions and chilli sauce; cook, stirring, until mixture is browned. Add bok choy, sauces and basil; cook, stirring, until bok choy is just tender.

Serve immediately, over steamed rice, if desired.

Microwave Suitable
Per serve fat 6g; fibre 3g; kj 827

34 chicken kumara

stir-fry

500g chicken thigh
fillets, chopped

cooking-oil spray

1 clove garlic, crushed

1 medium (150g)
onion, chopped
roughly

1 small (250g) kumara,
chopped

$1/4$ bunch (250g)
silverbeet, chopped
roughly

$1/2$ teaspoon sesame
oil

1 teaspoon cornflour

1 teaspoon chicken
stock powder

1 cup (250ml) water

Stir-fry chicken, in batches, in heated oiled wok
or large pan until browned all over. Add garlic,
onion and kumara; stir-fry until kumara is just
tender. Return chicken to same pan with
silverbeet, sesame oil and blended cornflour,
stock powder and water; stir over heat until
mixture boils and thickens.

Per serve fat 7g; fibre 2g; kj 899

36 chicken, kumara and
fettuccine stir-fry

Combine chicken, ¹/₄ cup of the basil, vinegar, juice, sugar and garlic in large bowl. Cover; refrigerate 3 hours or overnight.

Drain chicken; reserve marinade. Cook pasta in large pan of boiling water, uncovered, until just tender; drain. Boil, steam or microwave kumara until almost tender; drain.

Heat oil in wok or large pan; stir-fry onion until soft. Remove from pan. Stir-fry chicken, in batches, in same pan until browned. Add kumara; stir-fry 3 minutes.

Return chicken and onion to same pan with reserved marinade, pasta and snow peas; stir-fry until marinade boils. Sprinkle with remaining basil.

3 (500g) chicken breast fillets, sliced

¹/₃ cup shredded fresh basil leaves

¹/₄ cup (60ml) white wine vinegar

2 tablespoons lemon juice

1 teaspoon sugar

3 cloves garlic, crushed

300g coloured fettuccine pasta

1 small (250g) kumara, sliced

1 tablespoon olive oil

1 large (200g) onion, sliced

150g snow peas, sliced

Microwave Kumara suitable
Per serve fat 9g; fibre 5g; kj 2169

wedges

2 medium (400g)
potatoes, peeled

1 small (250g)
kumara, peeled

1 egg white, beaten
lightly

$^1/_4$ teaspoon chilli
powder

$^1/_4$ teaspoon ground
black pepper

$^1/_4$ cup (15g) dry-
packed sun-dried
tomatoes

$^1/_2$ teaspoon chopped
fresh rosemary

4 (680g) chicken
breast fillets

lemon garlic beans

200g green beans

1 teaspoon lemon
juice

1 clove garlic, crushed

Cut each potato into 6 wedges. Cut kumara into 1cm slices, cut slices in half. Place potato and kumara in baking paper-lined baking dish; brush all over with combined egg white, chilli and pepper. Bake, uncovered, in moderately hot oven 40 minutes.

Meanwhile, place tomatoes in heatproof bowl, cover with boiling water, stand 5 minutes; drain. Chop tomatoes finely; stir in rosemary. Spread tomato mixture over chicken. Place chicken on wire rack in another baking dish; bake, uncovered, in the oven with potatoes, about 20 minutes or until tender. Total cooking time for potatoes is 1 hour.

Lemon Garlic Beans Boil beans until tender; drain. Return to pan or dish, stir in juice and garlic.

Per serve fat 4g; fibre 4g; kj 1290

38 chicken and sugar snap pea
stir-fry

2 teaspoons peanut oil

1 medium (150g) onion, chopped

1 medium (200g) red capsicum, sliced

100g sugar snap peas

3 (500g) chicken breast fillets, sliced finely

2 teaspoons cornflour

2/3 cup (160ml) chicken stock

1 tablespoon soy sauce

Heat half the oil in wok; stir-fry onion and capsicum over high heat until onion is just soft. Add peas; stir-fry further 1 minute. Remove vegetables from wok.

Heat remaining oil in wok; stir-fry chicken, in batches, over high heat until browned and cooked through. Return chicken and vegetables to wok. Add blended cornflour, stock and soy sauce; stir over heat until mixture boils and thickens slightly.

Per serve fat 5g; fibre 2g; kj 826

warm chicken
and nectarine salad

2 medium (360g) oranges

2 medium (380g) tomatoes

2 medium (340g) nectarines

cooking-oil spray

4 (680g) chicken breast fillets

2 tablespoons red wine
vinegar

1 small mignonette lettuce

1 small butter lettuce

orange yogurt dressing

2 tablespoons low-fat yogurt

$1/4$ cup (60ml) orange juice

2 tablespoons sour light cream

2 teaspoons chopped fresh mint leaves

1 tablespoon chopped fresh chives

Using a vegetable peeler, peel rind thinly from oranges, avoiding white pith; cut rind into thin strips. Halve tomatoes and nectarines and cut into thin wedges.

Cook chicken in heated oiled non-stick pan until browned both sides and cooked through; slice lengthways. Add vinegar and rind to same pan; simmer, uncovered, 30 seconds. Top torn lettuce leaves with tomatoes, nectarines and chicken; drizzle with rind mixture. Serve warm chicken and nectarine salad with Orange Yogurt Dressing.

Orange Yogurt Dressing Combine all ingredients in bowl; mix well. Cover; refrigerate 30 minutes.

Per serve fat 7g; fibre 7g; kj 1314

salad

4 (680g) chicken breast fillets, sliced

1 small (300g) bulb fennel, sliced finely

1/2 cup (80g) black olives

3 green onions, chopped

2 medium (360g) oranges, segmented

1 small cos lettuce

dressing

1/2 cup (125ml) orange juice

2 tablespoons red wine vinegar

2 teaspoons olive oil

1 teaspoon sugar

Cook chicken in heated large non-stick pan, stirring, until browned both sides and cooked through.

Combine chicken, fennel, olives, onions, oranges and Dressing in bowl; toss gently. Serve chicken mixture on lettuce leaves.

Dressing Combine all ingredients in jar; shake well.

Per serve fat 7g; fibre 5g; kj 1205

coriander

ginger chicken

2 cloves garlic, crushed

1 teaspoon grated fresh ginger

1/4 cup chopped fresh coriander leaves

1/4 cup chopped fresh mint leaves

2 green onions, chopped finely

1/4 cup (60ml) soy sauce

2 teaspoons caster sugar

8 (900g) chicken thigh fillets

Combine garlic, ginger, coriander, mint, onions, sauce and sugar in bowl, add chicken, mix well. Cover; refrigerate 3 hours or overnight. Drain chicken, reserve marinade.

Cook chicken, in batches, in heated large non-stick pan, until browned all over and cooked through, brushing occasionally with reserved marinade.

Per serve fat 10g; fibre 1g; kj 1213

42 fruity chicken with herbed
couscous

1¹/₄ cups (310ml) water

20g butter

1¹/₂ cups (300g) couscous

2 tablespoons chopped fresh parsley

500g chicken thigh fillets, chopped roughly

cooking oil spray

1 tablespoon chopped fresh oregano

¹/₄ cup (60ml) fruit chutney

2 tablespoons dry white wine

1 tablespoon grated fresh ginger

1 clove garlic, crushed

1 teaspoon ground cumin

¹/₄ teaspoon dried crushed chillies

Bring water to boil in pan; stir in butter and couscous, cover, stand 5 minutes or until water is absorbed. Stir in parsley.

Cook chicken, in batches, in heated oiled large pan, stirring, until browned all over. Return chicken to pan with oregano, chutney, wine, ginger, garlic, cumin and chillies; stir over heat until mixture boils. Serve with couscous.

Per serve fat 10g; fibre 3g; kj 1955

mushroom, chicken
and asparagus risotto

2 (340g) chicken
breast fillets

1 stick celery, chopped

1 green onion,
chopped

1/2 small (35g) carrot,
chopped

1/2 teaspoon black
peppercorns

250g asparagus

2 teaspoons olive oil

1 clove garlic, crushed

1 large (200g) onion,
chopped

250g button
mushrooms, sliced

100g shiitake
mushrooms, sliced

2 1/2 cups (500g) quick-
cook brown rice

1 litre (4 cups) chicken
stock

2 cups (500ml) water,
approximately

100g enoki
mushrooms

1 tablespoon chopped
fresh parsley

Per serve fat 8g;
fibre 10g; kj 2641

Combine chicken, celery, green onion, carrot
and pepper in pan, cover with water; simmer,
uncovered, 15 minutes or until chicken is
tender. Remove chicken; strain liquid, reserve.
Cut chicken into thin strips. Boil or microwave
asparagus until just tender; cut into 4cm pieces.
Heat oil in large heavy-based pan; cook garlic,
onion and mushrooms, stirring, until onion is
soft. Stir in rice. Combine reserved liquid, stock
and enough water to total 2 litres (8 cups) of
liquid in another pan; bring to boil, keep hot.
Stir 2/3 cup (160ml) hot stock mixture into rice
mixture; cook, stirring, over low heat until liquid
is absorbed. Continue adding stock mixture
gradually, stirring until absorbed between each
addition. Total cooking time should be about 35
minutes. Stir in chicken, asparagus, enoki
mushrooms and parsley; stir until hot.

sandwiches

chicken and coleslaw roll-ups

2 cups (340g) shredded cooked chicken

1/4 cabbage (about 600g), shredded

2 medium (240g) carrots, grated

1/4 cup chopped fresh chives

1 cup (150g) dried apricots, chopped

1 cup (250ml) mayonnaise

1 tablespoon white vinegar

8 pieces lavash

Combine chicken, cabbage, carrot, chives and apricots in a bowl; stir in combined mayonnaise and vinegar. Place a spoonful of filling in the centre of each bread, roll up tightly and serve.

Serves 8

heavenly chicken-salad sandwich filling

1 bunch (1.5kg) celery

1.5kg chicken

2.5 litres (10 cups) cold water

1 medium (120g) carrot, quartered

1 medium (150g) onion, quartered

1 teaspoon black peppercorns

4 bay leaves

mayonnaise

3 egg yolks

2 tablespoons white wine vinegar

1 teaspoon Dijon mustard

1 1/4 cups (310ml) olive oil

Cut off celery base and top third of sticks; reserve trimmed centre sticks. Combine roughly chopped celery base and tops with chicken, water, carrot, onion, peppercorns and bay leaves in large pan. Bring to boil; simmer, covered, 50 minutes or until chicken is tender and cooked through. Remove from heat; when chicken is cool enough to handle, remove and discard all skin and bones. (Strain and reserve stock for another use.) Finely chop

chicken club sandwich

6 pieces freshly toasted bread
¹/₃ cup (80ml) mayonnaise
iceberg lettuce leaves
1 large (250g) tomato, sliced
*4 bacon rashers, fried crisply
or grilled*
*2 small (340g) chicken breast
fillets, pan-fried or grilled, sliced*

Spread the mayonnaise on the toast, place a lettuce leaf on one slice, top with tomato and chicken, then another slice of toast. Top with lettuce, bacon, chicken and tomato, then remaining slice of toast. Repeat with remaining ingredients. Serve with a dill pickle and potato chips.

Serves 2
The classic club sandwich is made with three pieces of toast and cut in half diagonally. It's a delicious sandwich if all the ingredients are freshly prepared: the chicken, bacon and toast.

chicken and reserved celery; combine with mayonnaise in large bowl, season with salt and pepper. Refrigerate chicken salad, covered, until ready to serve.
Mayonnaise Blend or process yolks, vinegar and mustard until smooth. With motor operating, gradually pour in oil in thin stream; process until thick.

This luscious mix of beautifully poached chicken meat and homemade mayonnaise is also delicious served as a salad, on lettuce with sliced tomato and a hard-boiled egg. This amount will make about 12 generously filled sandwiches.

46 chicken enchilada stack

2 cups (500ml) chicken stock

1 1/2 teaspoons cumin seeds

2 cloves garlic, crushed

600g chicken breast fillets

5 x 20cm round flour tortillas

450g can refried beans

1 1/4 cups (250g) low-fat ricotta cheese

spicy tomato sauce

2 x 400g can tomatoes

1 clove garlic, crushed

2 tablespoons chopped fresh coriander leaves

1/2 teaspoon chopped fresh red chilli

Combine stock, cumin, garlic and chicken in large pan, bring to boil; simmer, covered, about 15 minutes or until chicken is tender, turning once during cooking. Drain chicken; strain stock, reserving 1 cup (250ml) stock for sauce, finely chop chicken.

Spread 4 tortillas with refried beans and 1 cup (200g) of the cheese. Pour 1/3 cup (80ml) Spicy Tomato Sauce onto ovenproof serving plate. Top with 1 prepared tortilla, sprinkle with 1/4 of the chicken. Repeat stacking with remaining sauce, tortillas and chicken, ending with tortilla, remaining sauce and remaining cheese. Bake, uncovered, in moderately hot oven about 30 minutes or until hot. Serve cut into wedges.

Spicy Tomato Sauce Combine undrained crushed tomatoes with remaining ingredients and reserved chicken stock in medium pan; simmer, uncovered, about 20 minutes or until reduced to 2 cups (500ml).

Per serve fat 15g; fibre 10g; kj 2414

48 saucy chicken balls with spaghetti

You will need to cook about 1/3 cup (65g) white rice for this recipe.

800g lean minced chicken

1 medium (150g) onion, chopped finely

2 tablespoons grated parmesan cheese

1/2 cup (35g) stale breadcrumbs

1 cup cooked white rice

1 tablespoon chopped fresh basil leaves

500g wholemeal spaghetti

2 medium (300g) onions, chopped, extra

1 1/2 cups (375ml) chicken stock

2 x 500ml bottles tomato pasta sauce

1 tablespoon chopped fresh parsley

Combine chicken, onion, cheese, breadcrumbs, rice and basil in large bowl; mix well. Roll rounded tablespoons of mixture into balls, place on tray, cover, refrigerate 1 hour. Cook pasta in large pan of boiling water, uncovered, until just tender; drain.

Combine extra onions and 1/4 cup (60ml) of the stock in large pan; cook, stirring, until onions are soft. Add chicken balls; cook, covered, about 10 minutes. Add remaining stock and sauce; simmer, covered, 5 minutes. Add parsley; simmer, uncovered, further 10 minutes. Serve sauce with pasta; sprinkle with extra parsley and grated parmesan cheese, if desired.

Freeze Uncooked chicken balls suitable

Per serve fat 15g; fibre 23g; kj 3727

chicken and
baby corn

2 teaspoons oil

4 cloves garlic, sliced finely

2 small fresh red chillies, sliced finely

750g chicken thigh fillets, sliced finely

1 medium (150g) onion, chopped

1 medium (200g) red capsicum, sliced

425g can baby corn, drained, halved lengthways

10 leaves Chinese broccoli, shredded

1 tablespoon fish sauce

1 tablespoon soy sauce

1 teaspoon grated fresh ginger

Heat oil in wok or large pan; stir-fry garlic and chillies until browned lightly. Remove from pan. Add chicken to same pan; stir-fry in batches, until browned all over and almost cooked through. Add onion and capsicum; stir-fry, 1 minute. Return chicken to pan with corn, broccoli, sauces and ginger; stir-fry until heated through. Serve topped with garlic and chillies.

Per serve fat 11g; fibre 5g; kj 1216

50 thai-style chicken
patties

2 cups (340g) cooked chopped chicken

1 small (80g) onion, chopped

$1/2$ cup (125ml) mild sweet chilli sauce

1 teaspoon fish sauce

1 tablespoon peanut butter

$1/4$ cup (60ml) low-fat yogurt

1 tablespoon chopped fresh coriander leaves

$1^1/_3$ cups (95g) stale wholemeal breadcrumbs

cooking-oil spray

Process chicken, onion, 2 tablespoons of the chilli sauce, fish sauce, peanut butter, yogurt, coriander and 1 cup (70g) of the breadcrumbs until combined. Shape mixture into 4 patties, toss in remaining breadcrumbs; refrigerate 30 minutes.

Place patties on oiled oven tray, coat patties with cooking-oil spray; bake, uncovered, in hot oven about 15 minutes or until browned. Turn patties over halfway through cooking. Serve patties with remaining chilli sauce.

Freeze Suitable
Per serve fat 12g; fibre 4g; kj 1246

52 chicken salad
roll-ups

6 (650g) chicken thigh fillets

2 tablespoons honey

$^1/_4$ cup (60ml) teriyaki sauce

1 medium (150g) onion, sliced finely

$^1/_4$ cup (60ml) low-fat mayonnaise

4 large pocket pitta bread

2 cups shredded lettuce

1 medium (190g) tomato, sliced

2 tablespoons barbecue sauce

Cut chicken into thin strips. Combine chicken, honey and teriyaki sauce in large bowl; mix well. Cover; refrigerate 30 minutes. Cook chicken mixture and onion in heated large non-stick pan, stirring, until chicken is cooked through. Spread mayonnaise onto 1 side of each pitta bread, top with chicken mixture, lettuce and tomato; drizzle with sauce. Roll up pitta bread firmly to enclose filling.

Microwave Chicken mixture suitable
Per serve fat 11g; fibre 4g; kj 2122

chicken and

vegeroni bake

2 (340g) chicken breast fillets

1 cup (100g) vegeroni pasta

30g butter

8 green onions, chopped finely

250g button mushrooms, sliced

1/3 cup (50g) plain flour

2 cups (500ml) skim milk

1 cup (250ml) water

2 small chicken stock cubes, crumbled

1/2 cup (35g) stale breadcrumbs

1/3 cup (25g) grated parmesan cheese

1 tablespoon chopped fresh parsley

Microwave Suitable
Per serve fat 11g;
fibre 4g; kj 1680

Grill or steam chicken until tender, cool; chop roughly. Cook pasta in large pan of boiling water, uncovered, until just tender; drain.
Melt butter in large pan; cook onions and mushrooms, stirring, until mushrooms are soft. Stir in flour; cook over heat until dry and grainy. Remove from heat; gradually stir in combined milk, water and stock cubes. Stir over heat until mixture boils and thickens; stir in chicken and pasta. Spoon mixture into 4 x 1 1/2-cup (375ml) heatproof dishes, top with combined breadcrumbs, cheese and parsley. Bake in moderate oven about 15 minutes or until browned lightly.

54 coq au vin
kebabs

Soak bamboo skewers in water for 1 hour to prevent burning.

8 (900g) chicken thigh fillets

2 bacon rashers

8 (200g) baby onions

16 (about 160g) button mushrooms

1 teaspoon cornflour

1 tablespoon water

marinade

1 cup (250ml) dry red wine

2 tablespoons tomato paste

2 cloves garlic, crushed

1/2 teaspoon dried mixed herbs

1 small chicken stock cube, crumbled

Cut chicken into 3cm pieces. Combine chicken and Marinade in bowl. Cover; refrigerate 3 hours or overnight. Drain chicken; reserve Marinade. Trim fat from bacon; cut each rasher into 8 pieces. Thread chicken, bacon, onions and mushrooms onto 8 skewers. Grill or barbecue kebabs until cooked through, turning occasionally.

Combine reserved Marinade and blended cornflour and water in pan; stir over heat until mixture boils and thickens. Strain sauce and serve spooned over kebabs.

Marinade Combine all ingredients in bowl; mix well.

Freeze Marinated chicken suitable
Per serve fat 13g; fibre 2g; kj 1643

mango chicken

with macadamia

500g chicken thigh
fillets, sliced finely

cooking-oil spray

2 medium (340g) red
onions, sliced finely

2 medium (400g)
yellow capsicums,
sliced finely

1 medium (200g) red
capsicum, sliced finely

2 tablespoons dry
white wine

1 clove garlic, crushed

1 small fresh red chilli,
seeded, chopped

1 tablespoon chopped
fresh basil

2 medium (860g)
mangoes, sliced finely

250g rocket

1/4 cup (35g) chopped
macadamias, toasted

Stir-fry chicken, in batches, in heated oiled wok or large pan until
browned and almost cooked through. Add onions and capsicums to same
pan; stir-fry until soft. Add wine, garlic, chilli and basil; bring to boil.
Return chicken to same pan with mangoes and three-quarters of the
rocket; stir until rocket is just wilted. Serve remaining rocket topped with
chicken mixture and nuts.

Per serve fat 13g; fibre 7g; kj 1538

tandoori chicken
pizza

2 (340g) chicken breast fillets, sliced finely

2 tablespoons low-fat yogurt

2 tablespoons tandoori paste

1/2 cup (125ml) low-fat yogurt, extra

1/3 cup (80ml) hot mango chutney

1 large (300g) red onion

1 medium (120g) zucchini

2 tablespoons water

2 cloves garlic, crushed

1/3 cup (50g) unsalted roasted cashews

pizza dough

1 tablespoon (14g) dried yeast

1/2 teaspoon sugar

2/3 cup (160ml) warm water

11/2 cups (225g) plain flour

2 teaspoons olive oil

Combine chicken, yogurt and paste in medium bowl; mix well. Cover; refrigerate 3 hours or overnight.

Combine extra yogurt and chutney in small bowl; mix well. Cut onion into thin wedges. Using a vegetable peeler, cut zucchini lengthways into long thin strips. Combine water, onion and garlic in heated small pan; cook, stirring, until onion is just soft. Divide Pizza Dough in half, press half into 24cm non-stick frying pan; pinch edges decoratively, spread with half the chutney mixture, onion mixture, chicken mixture, zucchini slices and nuts. Cook, covered, over low heat on top of stove about 15 minutes or until pizza base is cooked through, then grill until topping is browned and chicken tender. Repeat this process with the remaining dough and toppings.

Pizza Dough Combine yeast and sugar in small bowl, stir in water, stand in warm place about 10 minutes or until frothy. Sift flour into medium bowl, stir in yeast mixture and oil, mix to a firm dough. Turn dough onto lightly floured surface, knead about 10 minutes or until dough is smooth and elastic. Place dough in lightly oiled bowl; cover, stand in warm place about 30 minutes or until doubled in size. Turn dough onto floured surface; knead until smooth.

Per serve fat 13g; fibre 6g; kj 2076

58 chinese
chicken salad

8 (900g) chicken thigh
fillets

1 teaspoon salt

2 teaspoons coarsely
ground black pepper

1/2 teaspoon five-spice
powder

5 Chinese dried
mushrooms

1 bunch (380g)
Chinese broccoli

2 sticks celery, sliced

4 green onions, sliced

1 1/4 cups (100g) bean
sprouts

1 medium (120g)
carrot, sliced

425g can baby corn,
drained, halved
lengthways

dressing

2 tablespoons salt-
reduced soy sauce

1 teaspoon peanut oil

1/4 cup (60ml) chicken
stock

3 teaspoons rice
vinegar

1 teaspoon finely
grated fresh ginger

1 clove garlic, crushed

1 small fresh red chilli,
sliced finely

Place chicken in single layer on wire rack on oven tray. Sprinkle one side with half the combined salt, pepper and spice. Grill until brown; turn, sprinkle with remaining spice, grill until tender; cool. Cut into pieces.

Meanwhile, pour boiling water over mushrooms in bowl, stand 20 minutes. Discard stems; slice caps finely. Cut leaves from broccoli stems, drop leaves and stems into pan of boiling water for 1 minute; drain, rinse under cold water, drain well. Combine chicken and vegetables in large bowl with Dressing.

Dressing Combine all ingredients in jar; shake well.

Per serve fat 11g; fibre 7g; kj 1392

chicken and lentil
cacciatore

8 (1.3kg) skinless
chicken thigh cutlets

cooking oil spray

1 medium (150g)
onion, chopped finely

1 clove garlic, crushed

2 x 400g cans
tomatoes

300g button
mushrooms, sliced

1 tablespoon tomato
paste

1 cup (250ml) chicken
stock

$1/2$ teaspoon dried
oregano

$1/3$ cup (65g) red
lentils

$1/2$ cup (60g) seeded
black olives

1 tablespoon drained
capers

2 tablespoons
chopped fresh parsley

Freeze Suitable
Microwave Suitable
Per serve fat 12g;
fibre 8g; kj 1684

Cook chicken in heated oiled large non-stick pan until browned all over, turning occasionally. Remove from pan.

Add onion and garlic to pan; cook, stirring, until onion is soft. Add undrained crushed tomatoes, mushrooms, paste, stock, oregano and lentils. Return chicken to pan; simmer, covered, about 30 minutes or until chicken is tender. Stir in olives, capers and parsley.

glossary

allspice also known as pimento or Jamaican pepper.

arborio rice large, round-grained rice especially suitable for risottos.

baby bok choy also called pak choi or Chinese white cabbage.

bacon rashers also known as bacon slices.

bean sprouts also known as bean shoots.

black bean sauce a Chinese sauce made from fermented soy beans.

breadcrumbs, stale one- or two-day-old bread made into crumbs by grating, blending or processing.

butter 125g is equal to 1 stick butter.

buttermilk low-fat milk cultured to give a slightly sour, tangy taste; low-fat yogurt can be substituted.

capsicum also known as bell pepper.

chinese broccoli also known as gai lum.

cornflour also known as cornstarch.

couscous a fine, grain-like cereal product, made from semolina.

curry leaves shiny bright-green, sharp-ended green leaves, use fresh or dried.

eggplant also known as aubergine.

endive, curly a salad leaf, also known as chicory.

fennel also known as finocchio or anise.

fillo pastry also known as phyllo dough.

fish sauce also called nam pla or nuoc nam; made from pulverised, salted, fermented fish.

five-spice powder mixture of ground cinnamon, cloves, star anise, Sichuan pepper and fennel seeds.

flour, plain all-purpose flour made from wheat.

garam masala a powdered blend of spices based on cardamom, cinnamon, clove, coriander and cumin.

ginger, fresh also known as green or root ginger.

gow gee wrappers wonton wrappers, spring roll or egg pastry sheets can be substituted.

hoisin sauce a thick, sweet and spicy Chinese paste made from salted fermented soy beans, onions and garlic.

jalapeno peppers fairly hot green chillies, available fresh or bottled in brine.

kaffir lime leaves aromatic leaves of a small citrus tree bearing a wrinkled-skinned yellow-green fruit; use fresh or dried.

kumara Polynesian name of an orange-fleshed sweet potato often incorrectly called a yam.

lavash unleavened bread of Mediterranean origin; also known as lahvoche.

lemon grass a lemon-smelling and tasting, sharp-edged grass; the white lower part of stem is used.

mesclun also known as mixed baby lettuce, salad mix or gourmet salad mix; a mixture of assorted lettuce and other green leaves.

onion

green: also known as scallion or (incorrectly) shallot; an immature onion picked before the bulb has formed, having a long, green edible stalk.

red: also known as Spanish, red Spanish or Bermuda onion; a sweet-flavoured, large, purple-red onion.

spring: have narrow green-leafed tops and a fairly large sweet white bulb.

oyster sauce a thick dark-brown sauce made from oysters, salt and soy sauce.

pancetta an Italian salt-cured pork roll, usually cut from the belly. Bacon can be substituted.

polenta a flour-like cereal made from ground corn (maize); similar to cornmeal but coarser and darker in colour; also the name given to the dish made from it.

prawns also known as shrimp.

rocket also called arugula, rugula or rucola; a peppery-tasting green salad leaf.

sambal oelek (also ulek or olek) Indonesian in origin; a salty paste made from chillies, sugar and spices.

sesame seeds there are two types, black and white; we used white in this book. To toast: spread seeds evenly onto oven tray, toast in moderate oven for about 5 minutes or stir in heavy-based pan over heat until golden brown.

shrimp paste also known as trasi and blanchan; a strong-scented, almost solid, preserved paste made of salted dried shrimp.

snow peas also called mange tout ("eat all").

spinach delicate, crinkled green leaves on thin stems; the green vegetable often called spinach is correctly known as Swiss chard, silverbeet or seakale.

sugar we used coarse, granulated table sugar, also known as crystal sugar, unless otherwise specified.

brown: a soft, fine granulated sugar containing molasses which gives its characteristic colour.

caster: also known as superfine or finely granulated table sugar.

palm: very fine sugar from the coconut palm. It is sold in cakes, also known as gula jawa, gula melaka and jaggery. Brown or black sugar can be substituted.

sugar snap peas small pods with small, formed peas inside; they are eaten whole, cooked or uncooked.

sultanas golden raisins.

tamarind concentrate a thick purple-black, ready to use sweet/sour paste extracted, from the pulp of pods from tamarind trees.

tandoori powder a flavourless mixture of yellow and red coloured powdered vegetable dye, available from Indian food stores. Substitute normal red food colouring if desired - not turmeric.

tomato

egg: also called plum or Roma, these are smallish, oval-shaped tomatoes.

pasta sauce, bottled: prepared sauce of crushed tomatoes and various spices and herbs.

paste: a concentrated tomato puree used to flavour soups, stews, sauces and casseroles.

puree: canned pureed tomatoes (not a concentrate); use fresh, peeled, pureed tomatoes as a substitute.

sun-dried (dehydrated tomatoes): we used the type sold in packets.

supreme: a canned product consisting of tomatoes, onions, celery, peppers, cheese and seasonings.

teardrop: small yellow, pear-shaped tomatoes, with the same texture and taste as red tomatoes.

tortilla thin, round unleavened bread originating in Mexico; can be made at home or purchased frozen, fresh or vacuum-packed. Two kinds are available, one made from wheat flour and the other from corn (maizemeal).

water chestnuts resemble chestnuts in appearance, hence the English name. They are small brown tubers with a crisp, white, nutty-tasting flesh. Their crunchy texture is best experienced fresh, however, canned water chestnuts are more easily obtained and can be kept about a month, once opened, under refrigeration.

wild rice from North America, this is not a member of the rice family but a grain from wild grass with a distinctive delicious nutty flavour.

yeast a 7g (1/4 oz) sachet of dried yeast (or 2 teaspoons) is equal to 15g (1/2 oz) compressed yeast if substituting one for the other.

yogurt low fat, plain: we used yogurt with a fat content of less than 0.2%.

zucchini also known as courgette.

62

index

facts and figures 63

These conversions are approximate only, but the difference between an exact and the approximate conversion of various liquid and dry measures is minimal and will not affect your cooking results.

Measuring equipment

The difference between one country's measuring cups and another's is, at most, within a 2- or 3-teaspoon variance. (For the record, 1 Australian metric measuring cup holds approximately 250ml.) The most accurate way of measuring dry ingredients is to weigh them. For liquids, use a clear glass or plastic jug having metric markings.

Note: NZ, Canada, USA and UK all use 15ml tablespoons. Australian tablespoons measure 20ml.
All cup and spoon measurements are level.

How to measure

When using graduated measuring cups, shake dry ingredients loosely into the appropriate cup. Do not tap the cup on a bench or tightly pack the ingredients unless directed to do so. Level the top of measuring cups and measuring spoons with a knife. When measuring liquids, place a clear glass or plastic jug having metric markings on a flat surface to check accuracy at eye level.

Dry Measures

metric	imperial
15g	1/2oz
30g	1oz
60g	2oz
90g	3oz
125g	4oz (1/4lb)
155g	5oz
185g	6oz
220g	7oz
250g	8oz (1/2lb)
280g	9oz
315g	10oz
345g	11oz
375g	12oz (3/4lb)
410g	13oz
440g	14oz
470g	15oz
500g	16oz (1lb)
750g	24oz (1 1/2lb)
1kg	32oz (2lb)

We use large eggs having an average weight of 60g.

Liquid Measures

metric	imperial
30ml	1 fluid oz
60ml	2 fluid oz
100ml	3 fluid oz
125ml	4 fluid oz
150ml	5 fluid oz (1/4 pint/1 gill)
190ml	6 fluid oz
250ml (1cup)	8 fluid oz
300ml	10 fluid oz (1/2 pint)
500ml	16 fluid oz
600ml	20 fluid oz (1 pint)
1000ml (1litre)	1 3/4 pints

Helpful Measures

metric	imperial
3mm	1/8in
6mm	1/4in
1cm	1/2in
2cm	3/4in
2.5cm	1in
6cm	2 1/2in
8cm	3in
20cm	8in
23cm	9in
25cm	10in
30cm	12in (1ft)

Oven Temperatures

These oven temperatures are only a guide.
Always check the manufacturer's manual.

	°C (Celsius)	°F (Fahrenheit)	Gas Mark
Very slow	120	250	1
Slow	150	300	2
Moderately slow	160	325	3
Moderate	180 –190	350 – 375	4
Moderately hot	200 – 210	400 – 425	5
Hot	220 – 230	450 – 475	6
Very hot	240 – 250	500 – 525	7

Food editor Pamela Clark
Associate food editor Karen Hammial
Assistant food editor Kathy McGarry
Assistant recipe editor Elizabeth Hooper

HOME LIBRARY STAFF
Editor-in-chief Mary Coleman
Managing editor Susan Tomnay
Editor Julie Collard
Concept design Jackie Richards
Designer Jackie Richards
Book sales manager Jennifer McDonald
Group publisher Jill Baker
Publisher Sue Wannan
Chief executive officer John Alexander

Produced by *The Australian Women's Weekly*
Home Library, Sydney.

Colour separations by
ACP Colour Graphics Pty Ltd, Sydney.
Printing by Dai Nippon, Korea.

Published by ACP Publishing Pty Limited,
54 Park St, Sydney; GPO Box 4088, Sydney,
NSW 1028. Ph: (02) 9282 8618
Fax: (02) 9267 9438.

awwhomelib@acp.com.au
www.awwbooks.com.au

Australia Distributed by Network Distribution
Company, GPO Box 4088, Sydney, NSW 1028.
Ph: (02) 9282 8777 Fax: (02) 9264 3278.

United Kingdom Distributed by Australian
Consolidated Press (UK), Moulton Park Business
Centre, Red House Rd, Moulton Park,
Northampton, NN3 6AQ. Ph: (01604) 497 531
Fax: (01604) 497 533 Acpukltd@aol.com

Canada Distributed by Whitecap Books Ltd,
351 Lynn Ave, North Vancouver, BC, V7J 2C4,
Ph: (604) 980 9852.

New Zealand Distributed by Netlink Distribution
Company, Level 4, 23 Hargreaves Street,
College Hill, Auckland 1, Ph: (9) 302 7616.

South Africa Distributed by PSD Promotions
(Pty) Ltd,PO Box 1175, Isando 1600, SA,
Ph: (011) 392 6065.
CNA Limited, Newsstand Division, PO Box 10799,
Johannesburg 2000. Ph: (011) 491 7500.

Healthy Eating: Chicken

Includes index.
ISBN 1 86396 092 9.

1. Cookery (Chicken).
I Title: Australian Women's Weekly.
(Series: Australian Women's Weekly
healthy eating mini series).
641.665

Cover: Marinated chicken vegetable salad,
page 30.
Stylist Vicki Liley
Photographer Scott Cameron
Back cover: Mustard and rosemary chicken
with artichokes, page 7.

mini books

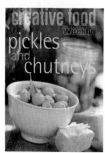